Really easy duets for young violinist
written, selected and edited by

PAUL DE KEYSER

CONTENTS

First published in 1991 by Faber Music Ltd
3 Queen Square, London WC1N 3AU
Music set by Sambo Music Engraving
Printed in England
Cover illustration by Penny Dann
Cover design by M & S Tucker

1 Mystery Melody

Can you spot the tune?

2 Minuet

Johann Krieger
(1649–1725)

3 Sadness

Bulgarian

Andante

4 All the Birds

German

5 Laughing, laughing

German

6 Air

Jean-Baptiste Lully
(1633–1687)

7 Hornpipe

Henry Purcell
(1659–1695)

8 Summer

Bulgarian

9 Folk Song

Bulgarian

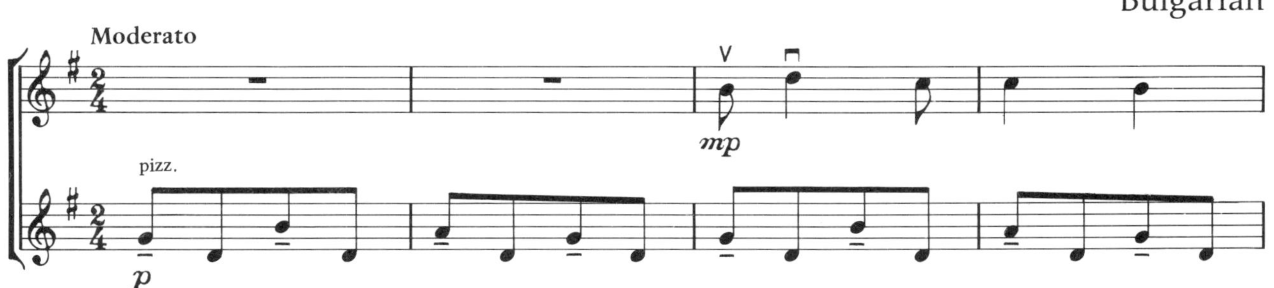

10 Aria (from Les Huguenots)

Giacomo Meyerbeer
(1791–1864)

20
24
cresc.
cresc.
f
f
29
34
1
1
2
0
3
39
sfz
sfz

11 Menuet

Jean-Philippe Rameau
(1683–1764)

12 Folk Song

Bulgarian

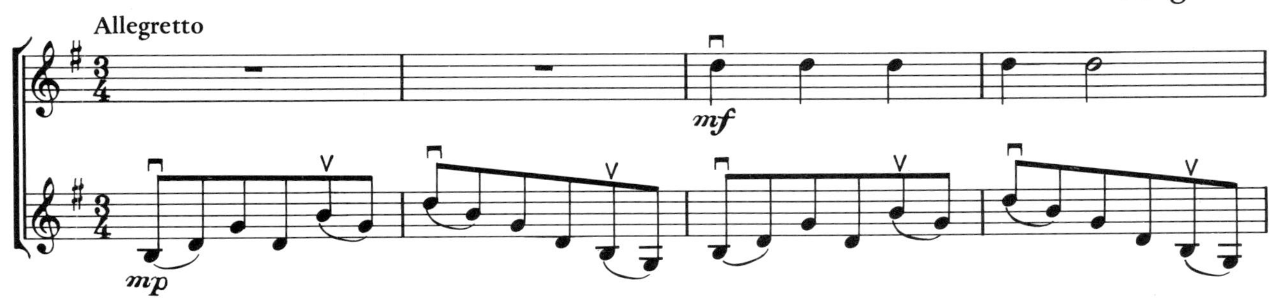

13 March

attrib. Carl Philipp Emanuel Bach
(1714–1788)

14 Krakoviak

Natalia Baklanova